Tyler's New Friend

Anne Kurkowiak

ROSEN
COMMON CORE
READERS

Rosen Classroom™

New York

Published in 2013 by The Rosen Publishing Group, Inc.
29 East 21st Street, New York, NY 10010

Book Design: Michael Harmon

Photo Credits: Cover, pp. 4, 5 Rob Hainer/Shutterstock.com; p. 6 Valery Shkloskiy/Shutterstock.com; p. 7 Nixx Photography/Shutterstock.com; p. 8 Andriy Maygutyak/Shutterstock.com; p. 9 RoxyFer/Shutterstock.com; p. 10 goran cakmazovic/Shutterstock.com; p. 11 Iakov Kalinin/Shutterstock.com; p. 12 RomanSo/Shutterstock.com; p. 13 JustASC/Shutterstock.com; p. 14 Dmitriy Shironosov/Shutterstock.com.

ISBN: 978-1-4488-8731-6
6-pack ISBN: 978-1-4488-8732-3

Manufactured in the United States of America

CPSIA Compliance Information: Batch #WS12RC: For further information contact Rosen Publishing, New York, New York at 1-800-237-9932.

Word Count: 88

Contents

This is Tyler.

He makes friends at school.

Tyler has a new friend.
Her name is Riley.

Tyler has a pet dog.
His dog is large.

Riley has a dog, too.
Her dog is small.

Tyler has a little sister.
Her name is Sarah.

Riley has a big brother.
His name is Mike.

Tyler likes the winter.
He likes cold weather.

Riley likes the summer.
She likes hot weather.

Tyler likes soft music.

Riley likes loud music.

Tyler and Riley are good friends.
Who are your good friends?

Opposites

large	small
little	big
cold	hot
soft	loud

Words to Know

brother

sister

Index